The Great American
Chili Collection

Edited By
Monte L. Melugin

Book Design By
Monte Albert Melugin

Aknowledgments

I would like to acknowledge the unending help of my son, Monte Albert Melugin, who without his assistance in the design and technical knowledge this e-book would have never been possible. He is my creative inspiration for whatever accomplishments I have made.

I also want to thank the many chili heads whose recipes, many of which can no longer be found, I have acquired over the last twenty-eight years. I am honored to bring them together in this collection.

Dedication

To my sons Christofer and Monte "Nunu" for supporting me in every endeavor I have ventured into. Also to my wife Maria, who has put up with more of my bull over the last forty-two years than any woman should ever have to.

Copyright

Table of Contents

Table of Contents Continued

Introduction

Growing up in the southwest, I developed a real fondness for all sorts of spicy foods, especially if they had overtones of Mexican cuisine. Even today, the words taco, tamale, enchilada, burrito, or quesadilla make my mouth starts to salivate. In fact, I can't think of any Tex-Mex dish I don't absolutely love. So it seemed only natural that I got hooked some twenty years ago on what has probably become my absolute favorite Southwestern dish, chili. I love to cook and eat chili. All kinds of chili. So when I was considering the subject for my first cookbook, the food that kept popping up in my head was chili.

I thought it would fun to put together a collection of great chili recipes developed by both novice and professional cooks from around our wonderful country. So within the following pages you'll find fifty-two chili recipes created by famous chefs and personalities like America's favorite weather man, Al Roker, and celebrity chef Michael Symon, as well as some recipes by lesser known, but fantastic cooks all the same. There are recipes from well know chili parlors and restaurants, award winning recipes from ISCC competitions, and even one of the first chili recipes ever published. Some of the recipes can be found in other publications and some are so obscure that they are no longer available, even online.

You'll also find the story of chili as we know it—how it came to the southwest and by whom, and how its popularity spread across this fine country. You'll also fine information about many popular chiles, both fresh and dried, to assist you in your quest to produce a great chili. And finally there's a list of ingredients and tools that every chilihead should keep on hand, so when you get the urge to cook up a pot of that wonderful elixer you won't have to make a special run to the market.

I hope you'll enjoy the following materials and cooking some of the recipes as much as I've had in preparing this, The Great American Chili Collection.

"Next to jazz music, there is nothing that lifts the spirit and strengthens the soul more than a good bowl of chili."
—Harry James

All About Chili, the Popular American Dish with Mexican Roots

There is one fact about the genesis of that popular, spicy concoction we call chili (or chili con carne) that should be cleared up right from the start—it did not come from Mexico. If there is any doubt of what the citizenry of our southernmost neighbors think of this dish, one needs only to consult the Diccionario de Mejicanismos, which defines chili as "detestable food passing itself off as Mexican, sold in the U.S. from Texas to New York."

Although there are many stories and legends about the origin of chili, research points to Texas as its most likely birthplace—San Antonio, Texas to be specific. And although not of direct Mexican decent, there is little doubt that this popular American stew is heavily influenced by Mexican spices and ingredients. After all, San Antonio was founded by the Spanish in the early 1700s. It is said that in an effort to quickly establish their presence, the King of Spain sent sixteen families from the Canary Islands (one of Spain's sovereign territories) to San Antonio to settle the area. In their attempt to replicate the much loved spicy, pungent stews of their homeland, these immigrants found it necessary to substitute their native meats, spices, berries, peppers, and other ingredients with those sourced from the local Mexicans and Indians. Thus chili was born. And while some ingredients may have changed over the years (beef instead of buffalo or wild game; domesticated chilies instead of wild peppers, known as "chiliquitas" for instance), the basic recipe for the dish remains the same today.

In the 1880s, a number of women known as the Chili Queens, started setting up stands in an area of San Antonio known as Military Plaza from which they sold chili (or "bowls o' red," as it was called) for ten cents, including bread and water. It wasn't long before word of these open air stalls spread and Military Plaza became a tourist attraction. In fact, so great was the Chili Queens' fame that the 1893 World's Fair in Chicago had its own San Antonio Chili Stand from which it introduced this southwestern elixir to the world outside the American West.

The reign of San Antonio's Chili Queens ended in September of 1937 when the local health department implemented sanitary standards requiring the Queens to adhere to the same health codes as brick-and-mortar restaurants. Although Mayor Maury Maverick reinstated their operating privileges in 1939, the health department developed even more stringent rules that were reapplied in 1943, and the Chili Queens disappeared from the city forever.

By the twentieth century, chili joints had made their debut throughout Texas and were spreading outside the state. During the 1920s and 1930s, "chili parlors" popped up across the Midwest and soon there was hardly a town anywhere that didn't have at least one chili parlor—often nothing much more than a room with a small stove, counter, and stools.

Some of the best-known chili parlors include Taylor's Mexican Chili Parlor which opened in 1904 on Main Street in Carlinville, the county seat of Macoupin, Illinois. Like most early chili joints, Taylor's is a small place with a counter and six wooden stools, a dozen well-worn tables, and plenty of framed photos and newspaper articles lining the wood-paneled walls. As one customer said, "People don't come here for the ambiance. They come for the chili."

Another of the Midwest's well known chili parlors is Big Ed's Chili Mac's Diner on Pine Street in downtown St. Louis. Big Ed's signature dish is called a "Slinger" and consists of two burger patties with slabs of melted American cheese, topped with hash-browns, two eggs, and smothered in chili. This chili-head's delight is still available today.

One of Texas' most popular chili parlors of all time was Bob Pool's chili joint which operated in downtown Dallas from the mid-1940s to the mid-1950s. Located across Main Street from Neiman Marcus, one of America's elite department stores, it was said that the store's president, Stanley Marcus, was not only a frequent diner but bought and shipped Pool's chili to friends and customers around the country.

Another Texas chili aficionado who is a must mention in any chili story is Frank X. Tolbert, historian, Dallas Morning News columnist, chili enthusiast, and co-founder of the World Chili Championship Cook-off in Terlingua, Texas. He also founded and operated the Original Frank Tolbert Chili Parlor in 1976 in downtown Dallas. By the time of his death in 1984, there were three locations, but by 2003, all had closed. In March of 2006, Frank's daughter, Kathleen, revived Tolbert's in a restored building in the historic district of Grapevine, Texas.

Today, chili can be found throughout America in a variety of styles. In addition to traditional Texas chili (chili con carne), which is thick, spicy, and never cooked with beans (but which are sometimes served on the side), Another popular chili is the rather mild Cincinnati-style chili, invented by Greek immigrants. There is green chili or "chili verde", a moderate to extremely spicy chili usually made with pork and popular in New Mexico. You also have white chili made with white beans and turkey or chicken meat, and finally vegetarian chili (also known as "chili sin carne").

In addition to the various styles of chili, it seems each region of the country has their own favorite way of serving chili. For example, there is Cincinnati's chili mac, or "four-way." This dish consists of spaghetti topped with beans, topped with chili, and finally cheddar cheese. Add diced onions and you have a "five-way."

In New Orleans, chili is prepared very much like Texas chili but served over slightly al dente rice. This is also the common way Hawaiians enjoy their chili—referred to there as "chili rice."

In Texas, where chili is the official state dish, it is usually enjoyed by itself, garnished perhaps with a dollop of sour cream, some chopped onion, and little cheddar cheese. And while the purists would never add beans to their chili, much of the time it is accompanied by a cup of pintos and a chunk of cornbread or tortillas.

No matter how you choose to enjoy your chili, enjoy it you should. Whether you prefer hot or mild, spicy or sweet, with beef, pork, or no meat at all, this collection of chili recipes has something to suit everyone's tastebuds. Just remember, chili can be just about anything you want it to be, except for one thing—it's not Mexican food!

Edited from the GrubAmericana.com entry, June 08, 2013

Guide to the World of Chiles

Chiles are the backbone of chili making and a key ingredient to any number of other Tex-Mex and Mexican recipes. The purpose of this guide is to introduce you to a number of chiles, both fresh and dried, in order for you to make an informed decision when choosing the ones that are right for your next pot of that delicious elixir we call chili.

Chiles are actually a fruit from the Capsicum genus, believed to have originated in South America and to have first been cultivated in Mexico. There are currently some 4,000 types of chiles, split into five domesticated Capsicum species: C. annum, C. frutescens, C. Chinense, C. baccatum, and C. pubescent. There are also 28 additional wild varieties.

It should also be noted that there is a distinct biological difference between chiles and peppers. Chiles fall under the plant genus Capsicum, while peppers are part of the Piper genus. So, although our society may refer to any of the pungent plants and fruits as peppers, they are an entirely different fruit than chiles.

It should also be noted that not all chiles are hot. Their heat is determined by the amount of capsicum oil they produce. A chile's heat is measured on the Scoville scale (SHU). For instance, a bell pepper (yes, it's actually a chile) is completely capsicum-free, has no heat, and comes in at zero Scoville units. On the other hand, the Carolina Reaper, one of the hottest chiles in the world, measures over 1.5 million SHU. The habanero (scotch bonnet) measuring 150,000 SHU, was the world's hottest chile until 2006. It is important to know Scoville measurements are approximate and can actually be a little higher or lower depending on the soil and climate in which the chile is grown.

ELEVEN OF THE MOST POPULAR FRESH CHILES

Shishito (*C. annuum*, 200 SHU) is a thin, dark green Japanese chili with a mild, slightly sweet flavor. Only about one out of 10 shishitos may have a little heat, but it is negligible. To eat shishito chiles, blister them first in a non-stick skillet, then squeeze lemon or lime juice over them, sprinkle with a little salt and enjoy.

Poblano chiles (*C. annuum*, 1,500 SHU), also known as **ancho** chiles in their dried form, are popular in Mexican cooking. Originating in Puebla, Mexico, they aren't the spiciest chilis you'll encounter but still contain a small amount of noticeable heat, which is more than enough for folks without much tolerance for spice. The ripened red poblano has significantly more heat and flavor than green poblanos. Roasted poblanos are a good way to add smoky flavor to Mexican and Tex-Mex dishes.

Mirasol chiles (*C. annuum*, 2,500 to 5,000 SHU) are most often found in their dried form referred to as **guajillo,** and are the second most common dried chile in Mexican cuisine. There are actually two varieties based on their size and level of heat. Guajillo pula is the smaller and hotter of the two, while the larger variety has a richer flavor and is less spicy. Mirasol chiles are more likely to be used in their guajillo form as a component in a Mexican or Tex-Mex dish than to be eaten on their own. If not using dried peppers, pick the freshest ones you can possibly find, since older fruit tends to pack less flavor

Fresno chiles (*C. annuum,* 2,500 to 10,000 SHU) These medium-sized chiles are often mistaken for jalapeño chiles but have milder heat and thinner walls. Developed in 1952 by Clarence B. Hamlin and named in honor of Fresno, California in the San Joaquin Valley, where they are a major cash crop. Fresno chiles can be used fresh or canned, but do not dry well due to their thick skin. Fresnos are delicious charred and added to romesco or minced and added to ceviche.

Jalapeño chiles (*C. annuum,* 6,000 to 8,500 SHU) A ubiquitous pepper loved across the U.S. and in Mexico, its fleshy skin can be sliced and added to just about anything. Jalapeños can also be marinated with vegetables and pickled like you see in escabeche. When ripened and smoke-dried, the chile transforms into chipotle peppers, which can be canned in adobo sauce or left dried and pulverized to a powder. The name jalapeño is Spanish for "from Xalapa", the capital of Veracruz, Mexico where the Chile was originally cultivated.

Serrano (*C. annuum,* 10,000 to 25,000 SHU) Originating from the mountainous regions of Mexico's Puebla and Hidalgo states, this is the second most used Chile in Mexican cuisine. Widely available in both green and red, these small pungent peppers should never be used in place of jalapeños, as they can pack almost double the heat. Serrano chiles are commonly used to make pico de Gallo and salsa.

Anaheim (*C. annuum,* 500 to 2,500 SHU) Mild, green, and about 6 - 10 inches long, the Anaheim chile pepper is named for the southern California city of Anaheim. Originating in New Mexico, the Anaheim was brought to California in 1894 by Emilio Ortega where it is grown commercially even today. In New Mexico the Anaheim pepper is referred to as "New Mexico Chiles", except when grown in the Hatch region where it is known as the popular **Hatch Chili Pepper.** Dried green Anaheim peppers are called "seco del norte". Dried red Anaheims are called California red or "chili Colorado."

Cubanelle (*C. annuum,* 100 to 1,000 SHU) Also known as the "Cuban pepper," this mild varietal of bell peppers is more elongated, with a thinner flesh and slightly wrinkled appearance. Cubanelles are 4-6 inches long, 2 inches wide, light greenish yellow in color, and turn bright red when fully ripened. Cubanelles are used extensively in the cuisines of Cuba, Puerto Rico, and the Dominican Republic, and are quickly becoming popular in other cuisines as well, because of their rich flavor and pretty colors Cubanelles are also called **Italian Frying Peppers.**

Habañero (*C. chinense,* 100,000 to 350,000 SHU) The habanero is a very hot variety of chili that originated from the Amazon. From there it spread to the Yucatan Peninsula of Mexico where they became an integral part of that areas food. Habaneros are typically ¾- 2¼ inches long with a color ranging from green to orange and red, although they may also mature to white, brown, yellow, or purple. The habanero heat, flavor, and floral aroma make it ideal in hot sauce, salsa, and other spicy foods. One should not confuse the habanero with the Scotch Bonnet. Though both varieties are of the same species and share similar degree of flavor, heat, and pungency, they are two distinctly different chilies.

Pequin (*C. annuum,* 30,000 to 40,000 SHU) Though the smallest of all chiles, (thus the name, which is Spanish for "small") the pequin packs quite a punch—five to six times hotter than jalapeños. Their flavor is described as nutty and citrusy. Originating from the Mexican state of Tabasco, pequin peppers are commonly used to make salsa or as a complement to a number of other dishes. Like most chiles, the pequin fruit starts out green and turns a brilliant red when ripe.

Tabasco (*C. frutescens,* 30,000 to 50,000 SHU) Another chile originating from the Mexican state of Tabasco, this pepper is best known for its use in producing Tabasco sauce and peppered vinegar. Its tapered fruit measures about 4 cm long and is initially a pale greenish yellow, turning to yellow and orange before ripening to bright red.

TWELVE OF THE POPULAR DRIED CHILES

When deciding which chilies to use in your next batch of chili you will need to ask yourself a few questions. Are you using a recipe? If so, there is pretty much nothing more to consider.

If creating your own or altering a recipe, you'll need to decide what flavor profile the chiles you're considering will impart into your brew. Do you want it sweet, smoky, earthy, or fruity, or a combination of two or more of these flavors? You'll also want to decide how mild or hot you want your chili to be. And finally, which chiles do you feel will best provide the flavor you're looking for—fresh or dried?

We've already introduced you to a wide selection of fresh chiles, now let's look at some dried varieties and what each will bring to the pot.

Guajillo (2,500 to 5,000 SHU) In its fresh form, this chile is called a mirasol, as described above. The second-most used dried Chile in Mexican cuisine, the guajillo imparts a sweet, mildly smoky, astringent quality to your chili. Its delicate flavor pairs well with turkey or chicken chili as well as fish and wild game.

Chipotle Morita (2,500 to 10,000 SHU) These chiles are made from red ripe jalapeños which are dried, then lightly smoked. These dark red chiles, named after the Spanish word mojito, meaning "little blackberry" will add a sweet, smoky, somewhat chocolaty flavor and aroma to any beef, pork, chicken, or vegetarian chili. A close cousin, the **Chipotle Meco,** has a similar smoky flavor (but without the chocolate overtones) and comparable heat profile, making it a great substitute for the chipotle morata.

Aji Paprika (100 to 500 SHU) If you're looking for a smoky, yet extremely reserved chile, the reddish orange aji paprika (hailing from Mexico and South America) will fill the bill. Its sweet, tobacco-y, orange-y overtones go great in a turkey, chicken or vegetarian chili.

Mulato (1,000 to 1,500 SHU) This is one of two varieties of dried poblano chiles. Mulato peppers are poblanos that have been left on the vine until they turn brown before drying, whereas anchos are poblanos that are picked when red and sun dried. The mulato is flat, wrinkled, and always brownish black in color, with a sweet, smoky, chocolatey or licorice flavor with cherry, coffee, and tobacco undertones. This chile can be used in any chili but is at its best when paired with beef or turkey.

Ancho (1,000 to 1,500 AHU) The ancho chile is the sun-dried form of the ripened red poblano, and one of the most popular in Mexican cuisine. It along with the mulato and pasilia make up what is known as the "holy trinity" of chiles. Mildly sweet with a complex fruity plum-like flavor, tobacco-y back notes

and a chocolatey, earthy bitterness, ancho chiles won't overpower dishes with too much heat. They were bred for flavor rather than heat. Traditionally pureed and used in sauces, anchos also add interest to soups, salsa, and chili.

Pasilla de Oaxaca (15,000 to 25,000 SHU) These popular chiles are a major agricultural crop of the Mexican state of Oaxaca, where they are farmed on small-holding properties called ayuuk (pronounced "au-YOOK"). How they're clean and dried is a well-protected secret by the locals. Pasilla de Oaxaca chiles have a deep, smoky flavor with hints of fruit and tobacco, and a heat that lingers. The are great in a beef or black bean vegetarian chili. One whole chile will produce about two teaspoons of powder when ground.

Pasilla Negro (1,000 to 1,500 SHU) The Pasilla Negro chile originated in Mexico and Peru. Its name, Pasilla (pronounced "pah-SEE-yah"), means "little raisin" because of its dark, wrinkled skin. Its flavor is woody, rich and fruity, with notes of chocolate, prunes, or raisins, making it a great base for all kinds of chili. They're also good for making mole and enchilada sauce. They can also be ground into chili powder—one pasilla will make one tablespoon of pasilla negro chile powder.

Cascabel (1,000 to 2,500 SHU) Cascabels, also know at "rattlers", are thought to have originated in Mexico, although exactly where is not clear. Their nickname comes from the tendency of loose seeds to rattle inside the dried cascabel when it is shaken. Fresh cascabels are a chubby, round pepper 2-3 cm in diameter, called chile bola ("ball chili" in Spanish), with a color range from green to red, that darkens to a deep reddish-brown when dried. Cascabels are a bit acidic, slightly smoky and woody with undertones of nuts and tobacco. These chiles add a friendly, mild level of heat to any beef or vegetarian chili.

Pequin (30,000 to 60,000 SHU) These chiles are among the tiniest in the Capsicum annuum species, measuring about ½-inch long and ¼-inch wide. But don't be fooled by their size, as these chiles pack a powerful punch. Dried pequin peppers offer a mellow, nutty flavor, with hints of citrus, and smoky undertones. This chile is great in chicken or seafood chili.

New Mexico Chile (800 to 1,400 SHU) Fresh New Mexico chiles are known by a number of names—Anaheim peppers (see above), red chile, Hatch chile, or Pueblo Chile. They are mild chiles, originally grown in the 1500s in the Spanish colony of Santa Fe de Nuevo Mexico, the area known today as New Mexico. Possessing a sweet, earthy flavor with hints of acidity, weediness and cherry undertones, New Mexico chiles bring a mild heat to chicken, turkey, or pork chili.

Smoked Red Serrano (8,000 to 18,000 SHU) Serrano pepper the second most commonly used chiles in Mexico, preceded only by the jalapeño chile. When fully ripened these chiles are smoked, then dried to provide a well-rounded, slightly smoky flavor that is crisp and spicy, with citrus under-tones. Smoked red serranoes are generally ground into a chili powder used to season turkey, beef, game stews and chili.

Puya (5,000 to 10,000 SHU) These medium-hot chiles go by the same name whether fresh or dried. Measuring about 3 to 4 inches long and ¼-inch at the shoulder, puya chiles are often mistaken for guajillo chiles, but are a little smaller and a bit hotter. Puya chiles have a light, fruity flavor, with hints of licorice and cherries. They go great in beef or black bean chili.

FOUR CHILES CREATED MORE FOR HEAT THAN FLAVOR

While most chiles bring one of four flavor profiles (sweet, fruity, smoky, or earthy) to chili and other Southwestern and Mexican dishes, others are more unassuming and are used primarily to deliver heat. Here are four such chiles.

Chiltepin (50,000 to 100,000 SHU) Thought to be the first domesticated chile in Central-Eastern Mexico, dating as far back as 9,000 BC, the tiny oval chiltepin chiles look more like small orange-red berries than a pepper. Considered to be crazy-hot, in Mexico the chiltepin are often called "arrebatado," which translates to "violent" or rapid", alluding to the fact that their intense heat disappears very quickly. The chiltepin flavor profile is a sharp, smoky, earthy bite with an upfront heat that quickly dissipates, making it best to add them at the end of cooking

Habanero (150,000 to 350,000 SHU) Although dried habanero chiles share the same flavor profile (pungent with notes of coconut, papaya, and berry) as the fresh variety, they also share the same incredibly severe heat. In fact, dried habaneros tend to feel hotter since capsaicin is not water soluble and therefore does not evaporate as the chile is dried, but concentrates instead. It is advised that you add dried habaneros to your chili in small doses.

De Arbol (15,000 to 30,000 SHU) Chiles de Arbol originated and remain an important agricultural product in the Mexican state of Jalisco, located along its western coast. Also known as cola de rata ("rat tail") or pico de pajaro ("birds beak") due to their shape, this dark, woody stemmed chile has an acidic, grassy, nutty flavor, though they are bred more for heat than flavor. And while the de Arbol is considered a hot chile, it falls at the lower end of the scale. This chile is ideal for long simmering times due to its thick, tough skin.

Japones (15,000 - 30,000 SHU) Japones chiles (pronounced ha-po-NAYS) originated in Indi and are one of the most common dried chiles. They are also known as hontaka, santaka, and oriental chiles. Japones do not have a complex flavor, but offer a clean, sharp, neutral taste, as to let the flavor of other spices like garlic a cilantro come through. They are primarily used for heat, although like chiles de arbol, they are at the lower end of the scale and are ideal to use as part of your chili base to infuse some heat.

The world of chiles is vast, with many types from which to choose. To add to this already confusing issue, most chiles are available in several forms—fresh, dried, powdered, and paste. So how do you know which to use—which will best impart to your next pot of chili the flavor nuances needed to make it your own. While we've covered fresh and dried chilies, let's take a look at the pros and cons of the other two forms.

CHILI POWDER

While chili powder is certainly the easiest, most convenient path to a good pot of chili, it is not without its problems. Many times, ready-made, commercial chili powder contains other ingredients such as salt, cumin, and oregano, and are usually a blend of common chiles which may prevent you from highlighting the personalized flavor profile you seek in your brew.

If you feel you must use a chili powder, read the ingredients before buying. You want to pick one that contains only a single chile, for example Ancho chile, and no fillers of any sort. Better yet, purchase dried chiles of your choice, toast them, and grind them in a spice blender to make your own. If you don't use it all, store the extra in an airtight container for future use.

CHILI PASTE

Chili paste is, as the name implies, made from chiles. It may be a pure thick pulp that comes from grinding peppers in any number of ways, from mortar and pestle, a grinding stone called a metate, or any number of mechanical appliances. Or it may be flavored, mixed, and thinned while still retaining its name. In spite of these factors, chili paste should be considered a flavoring agent with a number of uses.

Chili pastes can be found and used around the world with different types and flavors. And since Mexico produces half of the world's chilies, it only makes sense that they have countless number of chili pastes.

All chili pastes have some degree of spiciness, heat, and flavor. Some more than others. For example, Ancho chili paste adds a subtle, rich heat and warming quality in any dish to which it's added, while Aji Amarillo chili paste adds a fruity, berry-like flavor with medium heat level. If you're looking for some serious flavor and heat, try Harissa paste, a spicy North African sauce, to add a smoky heat to your dishes.

Here again, you can make your own by toasting your favorite dried chiles, then soaking them in boiling hot water until soft, then removing them from the water (saving some to aid in the processing), and pureeing them in a food processor or with an immersion blender. Afterward you should store your paste in an airtight container in the refrigerator where it will keep for up to five days with no loss of pungency or flavor.

We hope you'll find this guide helpful as you seek to produce your signature chili, one that will make you the talk of the next cook off or impress your family and friends.

Fifty-Two of Our Favorite Chili Recipes

Al Roker's Chili

2 pounds chuck steak, cubed in bite-size pieces
1 pound hot Italian sausage, removed from casings
2 large onions, diced
12 cloves garlic, diced
1 Tablespoon ground cumin
1 Tablespoon paprika
1 Tablespoon pure chili powder
1 can (32-ounce) crushed tomatoes
1 can (16-ounce) pinto beans
1 can (16-ounce) Northern beans
1 can (16-ounce) dark red kidney beans
chopped scallions
sour cream
shredded cheddar cheese

1. Brown the beef and sausages in a large Dutch oven.
2. Remove the meat. Drain off the fat, reserving about two tablespoons.
3. Sauté the onions and garlic until translucent, about 7 minutes.
4. Add the cumin, paprika, chili powder, and tomatoes. Add the cooked beef and sausage back into the Dutch oven. Simmer mixture for about 1½ hours, stirring occasionally to prevent burning.
5. Add the three cans of beans, and simmer for another 30 minutes.
6. Serve with dishes of chopped scallions, sour cream and shredded cheddar cheese. Cornbread is great with this also!

Contributor: Al Roker

Chili Mac and Cheese

1 to 2 Tablespoons cooking oil
1 pound lean ground beef
1 large onion, diced (about 1½ cup)
1 Tablespoon minced garlic
1 cup canned white kidney beans, drained and
   rinsed
1 cup canned red kidney beans, drained and rinsed
1 can (14½-ounce) diced tomatoes
1 can (8-ounce) tomato sauce
4 cup chicken broth
1½ cup elbow pasta, uncooked
1½ Tablespoon chili powder
2 teaspoon ground cumin
1½ teaspoon coriander
2 teaspoon dried or ground oregano
1 teaspoon dried thyme
¼ teaspoon cayenne pepper
Kosher salt to taste
black pepper freshly ground to taste
1 to 2 cups shredded cheddar cheese
2 Tablespoons roughly chopped fresh parsley leaves

1.   Add oil in a large dutch oven, place over medium-high heat. Add ground beef, breaking apart with a wooden spatula, stir frequently until beef has been cooked through and browned. Drain excess oil if any. (To avoid draining fat use lean ground beef.)
2.   Stir in onions, thyme and garlic; continue cooking for about 3 to 5 minutes or until the onion wilted and aromatic.
3.   Add diced tomatoes, kidney beans, white beans, tomato sauce, and elbow pasta, followed by all the spices; ground cumin, coriander, cayenne pepper, ground chili powder, chicken broth, salt and pepper to taste.
4.   Stir everything to fully combine, bring to a boil. Lower heat to simmer, cover the pot and continue cooking for about 10 to 12 minutes or until the elbow macaroni is cooked. Start checking after 10 minutes
5.   Once macaroni has been cooked, stir in shredded cheese and mix to fully combine. Reserve half of the cheese to sprinkle on top of the dish. Place in heated oven and broil for about two minutes until slightly brown or cover pot for about 1 minute just until the cheese melts. Garnish with fresh parsley, if desired, and warm. Serves: 6

Contributor: Anonymous

NOTES

Make sure to drain off fat if you are using fatty ground beef for chili mac and cheese.

Store chili mac and cheese in an airtight container in the refrigerator for about 4 days. Microwave to reheat.

Freeze leftover chili mac and cheese in an airtight container for about 2 months. Thaw and reheat—it is best reheated in microwave. Chili mac and cheese can be made ahead by taking it off the stove when the pasta is still firm and saucy. Allow to cool at room temperature, then top with cheese. Put in an airtight container and freeze.

Cincinnati "Skyline" Chili

1 quart cold water
2 pounds ground beef
2 cups crushed tomato
2 yellow onions, diced
4 garlic cloves, minced
1 Tablespoon Worcestershire sauce
1 Tablespoon unsweetened cocoa
¼ cup chili powder
1 teaspoon cayenne
1 teaspoon ground cumin
2 Tablespoon apple cider vinegar
1 whole bay leaf
¼ teaspoon ground cloves
1 teaspoon cinnamon
1½ teaspoon salt
cooked spaghetti to serve chili over, optional

1.   Add beef and water to a 4-quart pot. Bring to a simmer while stirring until the ground beef is in very small pieces. Simmer for 30 minutes and add all the rest of the ingredients.

2.   Simmer on low, uncovered, for 3 hours. Add water as needed if the chili becomes to thick.

3.   Refrigerated the chili overnight, and the next day remove the layer of fat from top before reheating and serving. Serves: 6

Contributor: John Mitzewich

THE CINCINNATI "SKYLINE" CHILI ORDERING CODE

1-way: just the chili

2-way: chili served over spaghetti

3-way: chili, spaghetti, grated cheddar cheese

4-way: chili, spaghetti, cheese, and onions

5-way: chili, spaghetti, cheese, onions, and beans

All are served with oyster crackers.

Bob's Bitchin Chili

12 dried chile peppers (ancho, arbol, or japon
   variety) or to taste
1 teaspoon crushed pequin peppers or to taste
1 package Wick Fowler's 2-Alarm chili seasoning
4 pounds lean beef (or turkey), ground or cubed
2 to 3 cups water
1 cup dry red wine
5 fresh whole jalapeño peppers
2 Tablespoons masa trigo dissolved in ¼ cup water

1.   Remove stems and seeds from dried chile peppers. Place in a small saucepan and add enough water to cover. Boil 10 to 15 minutes. Reserve liquid; transfer peppers to a blender or food processor. Process to form a thick paste, adding enough reserved liquid for processing (or use plain water for a milder chili). Add all chili seasonings except masa trigo.

2.   Lightly brown meat in a Dutch oven. Add paste and enough water to barely cover the meat (or use reserved liquid from boiling chilies for a hotter chili). Cook for 30 minutes, then add wine. Cook for 30 minutes and add jalapeños. Cook an additional 30 minutes and add masa trigoas mixture.

3.   Serve with cornbread.

Contributor: Bob Phillips

Rockin' KB Chili

*3 pounds lean beef stew meat, cut into
¼-inch dice*
1 teaspoon kosher salt
1 teaspoon coarsely ground black pepper
¼ cup minced onion
4 cloves garlic, thinly sliced
¼ cup finely diced green bell pepper
1 medium jalapeño pepper, seeded and minced
2 cups prepared spaghetti sauce
1½ cups no-salt-added beef broth
½ cup dry red wine
2 teaspoons sugar
2 teaspoons sweet paprika
2 teaspoons ground cumin
1 teaspoon dried oregano
3 Tablespoons chili powder
One 3-inch cinnamon stick
½ cup dried apricots, cut into very thin strips
1 Tablespoon cornstarch
½ cup prepared Bloody Mary mix
*¼ cup coarsely chopped cilantro leaves and tender
stems*

1. Season the meat with the salt and pepper. Working in batches, cook in a large Dutch oven over medium-high heat until the meat loses its raw look. Do not drain. Reduce the heat to medium; add the onion, garlic, green bell pepper and jalapeño pepper and cook for several minutes, until they have softened.

2. Stir in the spaghetti sauce, broth, wine, sugar, paprika, cumin, oregano, chili powder, the cinnamon stick and the dried apricots. Once the mixture starts to bubble at the edges, cover and reduce the heat to medium-low.

3. Make a slurry by combining the cornstarch and Bloody Mary mix, then stir it into the pot. Cook for 45 minutes, stirring a few times.

4. Discard the cinnamon stick. Stir in the cilantro just before serving. Recipe makes 6 to 8 servings.

Adapted from Bob and Kathy Rosar, Amtrak food

Black Bean and Turkey Chili

2 Tablespoons extra-virgin olive oil
1 pound lean ground turkey (white meat only)
Salt and freshly ground pepper
3 garlic cloves, minced
1 medium onion, finely chopped
2 Tablespoons ancho chile powder
1 Tablespoon New Mexico chile powder
1 teaspoon ground cumin
1 can (14-ounce) chopped tomatoes
1 can (15-ounce) tomato sauce
1 can (15-ounce) black beans, drained and rinsed
4 corn tortillas

1.   In a saucepan, heat the oil. Add the turkey, season with salt and pepper and cook over moderate heat, breaking up the meat, until white throughout, 4 minutes. Add the garlic, onion, chile powders and the cumin and cook, stirring, until fragrant, 5 minutes. Stir in the tomatoes, tomato sauce and 1 cup of water; bring to a simmer. Cook over low heat, stirring occasionally, until thickened, 45 minutes. Add the beans and simmer for 15 minutes.
2.   Meanwhile, light a grill or heat a grill pan. Grill the tortillas over moderate heat until soft, 30 seconds per side; wrap in a towel.
3.   Season the chili with salt and pepper and serve with the grilled tortillas.

Contributor: Ronnie Killen

Burn 'em Up Chili

2 Tablespoons corn oil
2 onions, chopped coarsely
3 garlic cloves, minced
2 cups green bell peppers, chopped
3 pounds beef, coarsely ground
2 pounds lamb, coarsely ground
1½ Tablespoons salt
2 cups tomatoes, stewed & chopped
1½ cups tomato sauce
3 jalapeño peppers, cored, seeded, & diced
1 Tablespoon cayenne pepper flakes
1 Tablespoons sesame oil
1 cup beer
1 Tablespoon oregano
4 Tablespoons chili powder
¾ cup tomato paste

1.   Heat oil in a large heavy pot or cast iron Dutch oven. Put in onions, garlic, and bell peppers. Cook until onions are translucent. Add meat.
2.   Add the beer, tomatoes, tomato sauce, spices, peppers, and sesame oil. Bring to a boil. When boiling lower heat immediately to a simmer. Cook for 2 hours at a simmer, stirring frequently. Add the tomato paste and simmer for 30 minutes more. Serves: 8 - 10.

Contributor: Geraldine H. Sable

Chicken and White Bean Chili

2 Tablespoons vegetable oil
2 pounds chicken breast, boneless, skinless, cut
    into cubes
1 green bell pepper, diced
1 small onion, diced
2 jalapeño peppers, minced
2 cloves garlic, minced
1 quart chicken broth
1 jar (8 ounces) salsa
2 teaspoons chili powder
2 teaspoons ground cumin
1 teaspoon kosher salt
1 teaspoon ground black pepper
½ teaspoon paprika
⅓ teaspoon cayenne pepper
2 cans (15½ ounce each) white cannellini beans,
    drained and rinsed
¼ cup fresh cilantro

1.   Heat vegetable oil in a large pot over medium high heat. Sauté chicken, green bell pepper, and onion in hot oil until chicken is browned and vegetables tender, 5 to 7 minutes. Stir jalapeño peppers and garlic into chicken mixture; continue to cook until garlic is fragrant, about 1 minutes.

2.   Pour chicken broth over the chicken mixture. Stir salsa, chili powder, cumin, salt, black pepper, and cayenne pepper into broth; bring to a boil, reduce heat to medium-low and simmer chicken until tender and no longer pink in the center, about 20 minutes.

3.   Add beans and cilantro; cook until beans are hot and soft, about 10 minutes.

Contributor: Anonymous

Buzzard's Breath Chili

4 pounds beef (US boneless chuck)
1 can (8 ounce) tomato sauce
1 large onion (chopped)
5 cloves garlic (minced)
1 jalapeño peppers
5 Tablespoon chili powder
1 teaspoon ground cumin
½ teaspoon oregano
Salt (to taste)
2 cups beef stock (homemade if possible)
2 teaspoons paprika
2 Tablespoons cayenne pepper
*2 Tablespoons Masa harina (corn meal flour) or
    cornstarch dissolved in ¼ cup water*

1.   Take meat and chop into ⅜-inch cubes, removing all gristle and visible fat. Brown in an iron skillet (about 2 pounds at a time) until gray in color. Place in a large cast iron chili pot, adding tomato sauce and equal amounts of water. Add chopped onion, garlic, jalapeño peppers (wrapped in cheese cloth) and chili powder.
2.   Simmer for 20 minutes, then add cumin, oregano, salt and cayenne pepper to taste. As moisture is required, add homemade beef stock until amount used, then add water if needed. Simmer covered until meat is tender (about 2 hours), stirring occasionally. Then add Masa Harina to achieve desired thickness if needed. Add paprika for color. Cook ten additional minutes, correct seasoning to taste, discard jalapeños (if you want) and serve. A small additional amount of cumin enhances aroma when added in last ten minutes. Serves 4.

Recipe: CASI Chili Cookoff Winner 1971

Pools Brew Chili

2 pounds chuck tender roast, trimmed of
    fat and gristle and cut into small cubes
Vegetable shortening, such as Crisco, for
    browning meat
1 can (14-ounce) beef broth
1 can (14-ounce) chicken broth
1 can (8-ounce) tomato sauce
2 pitted dry-pack prunes
Water if required

SPICE MIX #1

1 Tablespoon paprika
1 teaspoon onion powder
1 teaspoon garlic powder
2 teaspoons beef granules
1 teaspoon chicken granules
½ teaspoon salt
1 Tablespoon New Mexico chili powder

SPICE MIX #2

2 teaspoons cumin
½ teaspoon garlic powder
½ teaspoon onion powder
½ teaspoon black pepper
½ teaspoon salt
2 Tablespoons mild chili powder
2 Tablespoons chipotle chili powder

SPICE MIX #3

1 Tablespoon Texas-style chili powder
1 teaspoon cumin
Salt to taste

1.   In a heavy medium-sized pot, brown the meat in a small amount of vegetable shortening over high heat. Drain off any excess shortening.

2.   Add beef broth, chicken broth, tomato sauce, prunes, and spice mixture #1. Bring to a boil, lower heat to medium, cover the pot, and cook approximately 2 hours. Remove prunes and add water if necessary. Cook mixture longer if meat is not yet tender.

3.   Add spice mixture #2 and cook 15 minutes over low heat.

4.   Add spice mixture #3 and continue cooking over low heat for an additional 15 minutes. Salt the chili to taste and serve hot. Yield: 4 Texas-sized servings.

Contributer: Bob Plager

Texas Red Chili

2 pounds coarse ground beef OR
2 pounds chuck roast, cut into ¼-inch pieces OR
2 pounds stew meat, cut into ¼-inch pieces
3 Tablespoons olive or vegetable oil
2 Tablespoons butter or margarine
1 large green bell pepper
1 large Texas yellow onion
1 can (8-ounce) tomato sauce
3 heaping Tablespoons chili powder
2 Tablespoons fresh garlic, chopped fine
1 green pickled jalapeño pepper
1 Tablespoon salt
1 Tablespoon coarse ground black pepper
6 cups water
3 ancho chili pods
1 Tablespoon ground cumin
½ cup all purpose flour

1. Heat the 6 cups of water in a saucepan. While this is heating, roast the ancho chili pods under a hot broiler for 10 seconds on each side. Remove the pods and when cool enough to handle, remove the stem and shake out any seeds inside. Place the pods in the water that has come to a boil, cover and remove from the heat. Let steep until later in the recipe.

2. In a large stew or chili pot, add the oil and butter. When hot, add one of the meats listed above. Brown the meat on a medium-high heat, stirring often. While the meat is cooking, peel the onion and dice into ¼-inch pieces and remove the stem, seeds, and membrane from the bell pepper. Also dice the remaining outer skin into ¼-inch pieces.

3. When all the pink has disappeared from the meat, add the onions and bell peppers and stir in well. Add the chili powder, cumin, salt, garlic and black pepper. Again stir well.

4. Add the flour a little at a time and stir to mix well. Reduce the heat to medium and let cook for 5 minutes. It will be normal for some of the flour to stick to the bottom of the pan. Add the broth that has the ancho chili pods in it *slowly*. Scrape the bottom of the pot with a spatula and now add the tomato sauce and the jalapeño pepper (remove seeds for less heat).

5. Stir to mix well, reduce to medium low and cook uncovered for 1½ to 2 hours, until the meat is very tender. Check and stir every 30 minutes, making sure to scrape the bottom of the pan to keep from burning. Remove and serve in a large soup bowl with crackers and/or jalapeño cornbread.

6. Optional toppings are finely grated longhorn cheddar cheese and fresh, raw, chopped yellow onion.

Contributor: Anonymous

Debdoozies Blue Ribbon Chili

2 pounds ground beef
½ medium onion, chopped
2½ cups tomato sauce
1 (15-ounce) can light red kidney beans
1 (15-ounce) can dark red kidney beans
1 (8 ounce) jar salsa
¼ cup chili seasoning mix
1 teaspoon ground black pepper
½ teaspoon garlic salt

1.   Place ground beef and onion into a large nonstick saucepan over medium heat. Cook and stir until beef is browned and crumbly and onion is translucent, about 10 minutes. Drain grease if desired.

2.   Stir in tomato sauce, light and dark kidney beans, salsa, chili seasoning, pepper, and garlic salt until well combined. Reduce the heat to low and simmer for at least 1 hour before serving.

Contributor: Deb

Mountain Heat Chili

3 medium onions, chopped
6 cloves garlic, minced
½ pound bacon, cut into pieces
2 ounces Gebhardt's chili powder
½ ounce dark chili powder
3 pounds chuck roast, cubed
Red pepper to taste
1 can beef broth
1 pound hot pork sausage
1 can green chilies, minced
½ teaspoon dried habanero chilies
1 teaspoon cumin
½ teaspoon coriander
1 can tomato sauce
1 can Rotel tomatoes
½ cups oregano tea
    (1 teaspoon oregano steeped in hot water 30
    min)
1 Tablespoon salt
4 drops Tabasco sauce

1.   Fry bacon in a large pot or large Dutch oven until just crisp. Add onions, garlic, and all chili powders. Sauté until onions are translucent, but not browned.

2.   Brown beef in large skillet, working in batches (if you crowd the pan, the heat will lower and the meat will not brown, but will steam in its own juices), adding sprinkles of red pepper while browning. Use a very small amount of broth if meat gets sticky, but just the smallest amount. Again, we don't want to steam the meat. Transfer each batch to Dutch oven after browning and stir.

3.   Brown pork sausage and green chilies. Add habaneros when sausage is just turning brown. When browned, transfer to Dutch oven. Cook over medium-low heat for 15 minutes, then stir in spices, tomato sauce, Rotel tomatoes, and remaining broth. Mix well. Raise heat and bring to a boil. When boiling, immediately lower heat to medium-low to maintain a healthy simmer. Cook for 30 minutes. Add oregano tea and Tabasco. Simmer, covered, for 15 minutes. Serves: 8

Contributor: Freddy Avin

Greek Beef Stew

3 Tablespoons olive oil
1½ pounds lean stewing beef, in 1 inch cubes
1 (6-ounce) can of tomato paste
3 Tablespoons red wine vinegar
2 cups water
¼ teaspoon ground cinnamon
2 medium onions, chopped
2 cloves garlic, crushed (or 1-½ teaspoons garlic
    powder)
½ teaspoon black pepper
¼ teaspoon ground cloves
2 teaspoons salt

1.   Heat oil in large stew pot. When oil is hot, but not smoking, add meat.
2.   Brown meat on all sides.
3.   Add tomato paste, vinegar, water, cinnamon, onion, garlic, pepper, cloves and salt. Bring to a boil. When boiling, reduce heat to a simmer and cook for two hours, covered, stirring occasionally. Serves 4 - 6.

Contributor: Cliff Lowe

Farmhouse Sausage Chili

1 pound pork sausage
1 large onion, chopped
1 celery stalk, diced
1 can (28-ounce) whole tomatoes, chopped
2 cups tomato juice or chicken broth or a mixture
    of the two
1 to 2 Tablespoons maple syrup or molasses
2 teaspoons ground cumin
1½ teaspoon powdered sage
½ teaspoon ground black pepper
3½ to 4 cups cooked red kidney beans, drained and
    rinsed

1.   Brown in a large skillet the pork sausage and the chopped onion.
2.   Toward the end of the browning, add the celery.
3.   When the celery is softened, add tomatoes, tomato juice or chicken broth, maple syrup or molasses, cumin, sage and black pepper.
4.   Simmer for 20 minutes.
5.   Add the red kidney beans.
6.   Simmer for 15 minutes more.
7.   Serve with sharp cheddar cheese, cubed and cornbread or buttermilk biscuits. Recipe feeds 4-6 people.

Contributor: Anonymous

Tim Horton's Chili

2 pounds ground beef
1 teaspoon olive oil
2-3 onions, diced
3 celery ribs, sliced
1 green pepper, diced
1 can (19-ounce) dark red kidney beans, rinsed and drained
2 cans (10-ounce each) mushroom pieces, drained and chopped
2 cans (10-ounce each) tomato soup, undiluted
1 can (28-ounce) diced tomatoes, undrained
2 Tablespoons chili powder, divided
1 teaspoon oregano
1 teaspoon salt
¼ teaspoon pepper
1 teaspoon granulated sugar
1-2 garlic cloves, minced, or 3 teaspoons garlic powder

1.   Preheat a large frying pan over medium heat. Add the olive oil and mix in the beef. Stir constantly until no longer pink, about 5 minutes. Transfer the beef into a large pot without draining.

2.   In the same frying pan, combine the onion, celery, and green pepper and cook until the onion is translucent, about 5 minutes. Season it with a bit of chili powder.

3.   Add the vegetables to the ground beef. Gently mix in the kidney beans, mushrooms, tomato soup, and canned tomatoes, careful not to squish the beans. Season with the remaining chili powder, oregano, salt, pepper, sugar, and garlic. Stir well to coat all the ingredients.

4.   Cover the pot and simmer over medium heat for 1 hour, stirring occasionally. Remove the lid and simmer for 30 more minutes or until thick, stirring occasionally. Serve and enjoy!

Courtesy of Tim Horton

Chocolate and Black Bean Chili

2 Tablespoons olive oil
1½ cups onions, chopped
4 garlic cloves, minced
1 celery stalk, sliced
2 jalapeños, minced
1 Tablespoon ground cumin
2 Tablespoons dry oregano
½ teaspoon ground cinnamon
1 pinch ground cloves
1 teaspoon ground coriander
1 Tablespoon chili powder
½ teaspoon ground black pepper
1 teaspoon salt
1½ cups bell pepper, chopped
2 cans (14½-ounce each) black beans, drained, rinsed
1 can (14½-ounce) diced tomatoes
1 Tablespoon fresh lime juice
1 Tablespoon soy sauce
¼ cup semisweet chocolate
Chopped scallion, cheese, or sour cream for serving

1.   In a large skillet, heat olive oil over medium heat. Add onions and garlic and sauté until onions become soft and translucent, about 10 minutes.

2.   Add the celery and chile, cover and cook for another five minutes more.

3.   Reduce the heat and stir in spices (cumin, oregano, cinnamon, cloves, coriander, chili powder, black pepper, salt) along with the bell peppers. Cover again and cook for another 5 minutes. Stir often to keep the spices from burning. If the pan gets too dry add a little liquid from the diced tomatoes, or some water.

4.   Next, add the black beans, tomatoes, lime juice (if using) and soy sauce. Let the chili simmer on low for 5 to 10 minutes until it thickens slightly and flavors combine.

5.   Stir in the chocolate. When chocolate has melted, taste to adjust the salt and pepper. Serve with toppings of your choice.

Contributor: Cosmic Blues

Dragon's Breath Chili

3 Tablespoons bacon grease or canola oil
2 Tablespoons unsalted butter
3 Anaheim chiles, roasted, peeled, chopped
3 poblano chiles, roasted, peeled, chopped
2 red bell peppers, diced
2 jalapeños chiles, minced
2 yellow onions, diced
1 head garlic, minced
1 pound boneless chuck, trimmed and cut into
　　¼-inch cubes
2 pounds ground beef, coarse grind
1 pound bulk Italian sausage
3 Tablespoons chili powder
2 teaspoons cayenne pepper
2 teaspoons ground coriander
2 teaspoons ground cumin
2 teaspoons granulated garlic
2 teaspoons granulated onion
2 teaspoons hot paprika
2 teaspoons kosher salt
2 teaspoons freshly ground black pepper
2 cups tomato sauce
1 cup tomato paste
12 ounces lager beer
1 cup chicken stock

1.　　Add the bacon grease and butter to a large stockpot over high heat.
2.　　Add the Anaheim chiles, poblano chiles, red bell peppers, jalapeño chiles and onions, and cook until caramelized, about 5 minutes. Add the garlic and sauté 1 minute longer. Add the chuck and brown, about 4 minutes. Add the ground beef and sausage and brown, stirring gently, trying not to break up the ground beef too much. Cook until the meat is nicely browned and cooked through, 7 to 10 minutes. Add the chili powder, cayenne, coriander, cumin, granulated garlic, granulated onion, paprika, salt and black pepper, and cook until fragrant, about 1 minute.
3.　　Add the tomato sauce and paste and stir to caramelize, about 2 minutes. Stir in the beer and stock. Add the kidney and pinto beans; lower the heat and simmer, about 2 hours.
4.　　Serve the chili in bowls over double-fried French fries and garnish with crackers, green onions and cheddar. Recipe makes 10 to 15 servings.

Courtesy Guy Fier

Texas-California Chili

*10 to 12 dried red chili peppers (re-hydrate over
night in 1 quart of warm water; weight them
down so they are completely covered with
water—retain water!)*
5 Anaheim (long, green) chili peppers
2 medium yellow onions
2 large Roma tomatoes (canned will work)
5 large cloves of garlic
⅓ cup pure chili powder—no chili mix
¼ cup cumin powder
1 Tablespoon cayenne pepper
1 Tablespoon red paprika
A healthy pinch of fresh oregano, smashed
12 ounces of beef broth
8 to 12 ounces tomato sauce (NOT tomato paste)
Salt to taste (kosher is best)
*2 pounds of "chili grind" chuck roast with some of
the fat left in*
2 pounds of pork loin, ground as above
1 cup of beer

1. Chop onion and garlic VERY fine.
2. Roast Anaheim chili peppers until the skin is completely blackened. (A small hand torch works great for this.) Strip off skin under running water. Split open and de-seed and de-vein them. Chop fine.
3. Blanch the tomatoes in boiling water until the skin comes off easily. Remove skin and de-seed them. Chop VERY fine.
4. Sauté all the above in olive oil over HIGH HEAT until onions are clear. Continuously stir—DO NOT BURN.
5. Pour beef broth into a 1 gallon stock pot (stainless is best), and add sautéed ingredients. Leave on low heat for now.
6. Brown the meats over HIGH HEAT in olive oil a little at a time, adding them to the stock pot as you go. Add tomato sauce.
7. Place the re-hydrated red chili peppers (remove most seeds and the stems) into a blender and cover with the retained water. Blend until it's all a liquid. Strain into the stock pot.
8. Add water as needed to keep everything covered. Add all spices to stockpot. Cook for 1½ hours at low heat, stirring often—DO NOT BURN! Add beer and cook another ½ hour
9. Taste test and season as needed. It should have a bite at about 10 seconds on the palate. The bite should last 20 seconds.
10. Add some good, homemade cornbread to make it a real pleaser!

Contributor: J. Lewis

Texas Truck Stop Chili

3 pounds beef brisket, trimmed and cut into ½-inch cubes
¼ pound bacon, diced
1 pound onion, chopped
1 Tablespoon cumin
3 Tablespoons chili powder
2 teaspoons paprika
1 teaspoon dried oregano leaves
Salt and pepper to taste
½ teaspoon dried thyme leaves
⅜ teaspoon ground cinnamon
4 large cloves of garlic, minced
1 can (13¾-ounce) beef broth
1 can (28-ounce) plum tomatoes in puree
2 dried chipotle chilies
1 cup water, optional
Additional chopped onion for garnish

1. Cut beef into ½-inch cubes. In Dutch oven, over medium heat, cook bacon until crisp. Remove; reserve. Remove all but 1 tablespoon drippings; reserve.
2. Over high heat, sauté beef in batches, adding drippings as needed. Remove to bowl; over medium heat, sauté onions in any remaining drippings 10 minutes or until well browned.
3. Meanwhile, heat skillet over medium heat. Add cumin; cook 1 minute or until very fragrant and toasted. Stir in chili powder, paprika, oregano, pepper, salt, thyme and cinnamon.
4. Stir seasonings and garlic into onions; sauté 1 minute. Stir in bacon, broth, tomatoes, chiles and beef, breaking up tomatoes with wooden spoon.
5. Heat chili to boiling; reduce heat. Partially cover; simmer gently 3 hours or until beef is tender, stirring frequently toward the end of cooking time to prevent sticking and adding water if necessary if mixture is too thick.
6. Remove and discard chipotles.
7. In bowls, serve chili topped with chopped onion. Recipes makes 8 servings.

Contributor: C. W. Huggins

Doomsday Chili

1½ Tablespoons olive oil
1 large onion, roughly chopped
5 to 6 cloves garlic, finely chopped
12 jalapeño peppers, seeded or unseeded (to taste),
    chopped
1-2 serrano peppers, chopped
2½ pounds lean ground beef
1 (15-ounce) can kidney beans
1 (15-ounce) can black beans
1 (8-ounce) can tomato sauce
1 Tablespoon paprika
1 Tablespoon cumin
1 Tablespoon garlic powder
1 Tablespoon oregano
1 teaspoon cayenne
Salt & freshly milled black pepper to taste

1.   Sauté the onions, peppers and garlic in olive oil in large, heavy-bottomed pot or Dutch oven until the onions turn golden.
2.   Stir in beef, breaking up with a wooden spoon, and cook until the beef is browned. When done, add all other ingredients to the chili mixture. You can transfer to a crock pot or continue to cook in the Dutch oven. If using a crock pot, cook for 6 to 10 hours. If staying on top of the stove, cook covered at a strong simmer for about an hour and a half. If more liquid is needed you can add water, beer, ale or red wine. Chili should be "to taste."

Contributor: Fred Avin

Fireman's Firehouse Chili

3 pounds ground beef
1 (15-ounce) can tomato sauce
1 cup water
1 teaspoon Tabasco sauce
3 Tablespoons chili powder
1 Tablespoon oregano
2 onions, coarsely chopped
1 teaspoon cumin
Garlic to taste, finely chopped
1 teaspoon salt
1 teaspoon cayenne pepper
1 teaspoon paprika
12 red peppers
4 or 5 chili pods
2 heaping teaspoons flour

1.   Sauté meat until browned.
2.   Combine all ingredients except flour in a heavy pot. Simmer 1 hour and 15 minutes.
3.   Thicken chili with mixture of flour and a little water. Simmer another 30 minutes.

Contributor: Richard Clements

Jeff's Hot Dog Chili

1 pound ground beef
⅓ cup water
½ (10-ounce) can tomato sauce
½ cup ketchup
2½ teaspoons chili powder
½ teaspoon salt
½ teaspoon ground black pepper
½ teaspoon white sugar
½ teaspoon onion powder
1 dash Worcestershire sauce

1.   Place ground beef and water in a large saucepan; use a potato masher to break apart beef.
2.   Stir in tomato sauce, ketchup, chili powder, salt, black pepper, sugar, onion powder, and Worcestershire sauce. Bring to a boil, then simmer over medium heat until beef is cooked and chili thickens, about 20 minutes.

Contributor: Orion 3

Simon Pearce Restaurant Chili

3 large onions, chopped
2 large green bell peppers, minced
4 garlic cloves, minced
2 cans (28-ounce each), Italian plum tomatoes
    with juice
2 (29-ounce each) cans tomato puree
¼ cup chili powder
1½ Tablespoon crushed red pepper flakes
2 Tablespoons ground cumin
1½ teaspoons dried oregano, crumbled
1 Tablespoon dried basil, crumbled
1 Tablespoon salt
2 pounds hot Italian sausage
5 pounds lean ground chuck
2 (16-ounce each) cans red kidney beans, drained
Sour cream, if desired

1.   In a large kettle cook the onions, bell peppers and garlic in the oil over moderately low heat, stirring occasionally, until the onions are softened. Add the tomatoes and their juice, the tomato puree, chili powder, red pepper flakes, cumin, oregano, basil, salt and simmer for 15 minutes.

2.   While the mixture is simmering, in a large skillet brown the sausage over high heat and drain it on paper towels. Cut the sausage into 1-inch lengths and add it to the tomato mixture. Pour off the fat from the skillet.

3.   In the skillet brown the chuck in batches, stirring to break up the lumps and with a slotted spoon transfer browned chuck to tomato mixture. Simmer the chili, stirring occasionally, for 60 to 90 minutes. Stir in beans. Can be made 2 days in advance, cooled and kept chilled and covered. Serve with sour cream. Recipe serves 12 - 14.

Contributor: Sally Challgren

Cry Wolf Chili

1 pound thick-cut bacon
3 pounds chuck roast, cubed
1 pound ground chuck
1½ pounds pork roast, cubed
5 cloves garlic, minced
3 large onions, chopped
1 can green chilies, chopped
2 teaspoons dry chopped habaneros
2 teaspoons dry red peppers
2 Tablespoons chili powder
1½ Tablespoons paprika
4 Tablespoons cumin
1 Tablespoons black pepper
2 teaspoons Tabasco sauce
2 Tablespoons Worcestershire sauce
1 can beef broth
1 can Rotel tomatoes
2 (15-ounce each) cans kidney beans
1 (15-ounce) can black beans

1.   Separate the thick strips of bacon and lay them in a large, COLD, heavy-bottomed pot or Dutch oven. For this proportion of meat, a pasta pot works well. Turn on heat to medium. Let cook very slowly until crisp. Remove with a fork or slotted spoon and drain on paper towels. Pour some of the drippings into a large skillet, leaving a small amount in the Dutch oven. Set the rest to the side for another use.

2.   Working in batches to avoid steaming the meat, brown meat and garlic in skillet. At the same time, sauté onions in Dutch oven just until soft and translucent. When onions reach this stage, add the browned meat. (The onions should be done before the meat—just keep adding.)

3.   Crumble the bacon and add to meat with green chilies and dried peppers, spices, sauces, stock, and Rotel tomatoes. Bring to a boil and, when boiling, lower heat to medium-low just to keep at a strong simmer. Cook chili, partially covered, for 2 hours. Add beans and simmer chili another 15 minutes. Serves 10 - 12 and freezes well.

Contributor: Anonymous

Chili Con Carne

1 Tablespoon olive oil
3 garlic cloves, minced
1 onion, diced
1 red bell pepper, diced
1 pound ground beef
3 Tablespoons tomato paste
1 can (28-ounce) crushed tomatoes
1 can (14½-ounce) red kidney beans, drained and
    rinsed
1½ teaspoon brown sugar
1½ cups beef broth
Salt and pepper to taste

SPICE MIX

1½ teaspoons cayenne pepper
4 teaspoons paprika
5 teaspoons ground cumin
2 teaspoons garlic powder
2 teaspoons onion powder
2 teaspoons dried oregano

1.   Heat oil in a large skillet over medium-high heat. Add garlic and onion, cook for 1 minute, then add capsicum and cook for 2 minutes until onion is translucent.

2.   Turn heat up to high and add beef. Cook, breaking it up as you go, until mostly browned. Add Spice Mix. Cook until beef is browned all over. (This step helps release extra flavor from the spices.)

3.   Add remaining ingredients, with 1½ cups stock. Bring to simmer, then cook 20 to 40 minutes, uncovered, on medium low heat so it's bubbling gently.

4.   Adjust salt and pepper to taste just before serving.

5.   Serve over rice, or ladle into bowls and serve with corn chips or warm tortillas on the side with sour cream, cheese and coriander. Serves 6.

Adapted from recipe by Nagi

Mrs Day's Vintage Chili Soup

1 pound hamburger steak
2 Tablespoons butter or suet
1 teaspoon salt
¼ teaspoon black pepper
½ teaspoon Mexene Chili powder
1 quart strained tomatoes
1 can chili or red kidney beans
2 medium onions

1.   Add water to make desired strength, and cook slowly for ½ hour, or until flavors are well blended.

Contributor: F. E. Day

NOTE

This recipe comes from page 10 of the Newton Cook Book, published 1914 by The Ladies Aid Society, Methodist Episcopal Church.

Pedernales River Chili

4 pounds ground beef
1 large onion, chopped
2 garlic cloves, minced
1 teaspoon dried oregano
1 teaspoon ground cumin
2 Tablespoons chile powder, or to taste
1½ cups canned tomatoes, cut up
2 to 6 dashes hot sauce, or to taste
Salt to taste

1.   Cook the meat, onion and garlic in a Dutch oven over medium heat, stirring, until lightly browned. Stir in the oregano, cumin, chile powder, tomatoes, hot sauce, salt and 2 cups hot water. Bring to a boil, lower heat and simmer, covered, for about 1 hour, skimming off the fat as it cooks. Makes 12 servings.

Adapted from Lady Bird Johnson

NOTE

This chili was named after the location of President Lyndon B. Johnson's Texas Hill Country ranch. Mrs. Lady Bird Johnson had cards printed with the "Pedernales River Chili" recipe and mailed it to the thousands of requests received from around the country.

West Texas Chuckwagon Chili

3 pounds ground venison with suet (or a 3 pound lean chuck roast, diced into ½-inch bits)
6 cloves of garlic, minced
1 Tablespoon chili powder (add more, if you dare)
3 Tablespoons oregano, dried
3 Tablespoons cumin, ground
½ to 1½ teaspoons cayenne (this is the heat - adjust up or down)
1 to 2 teaspoon salt (kosher or coarse sea salt)
⅓ cup corn meal (coarse is really good)
⅓ cup cold, fresh water
1 to 1½ quarts cold, fresh water

1.   Brown the meat—dry it out a bit. Add the chili powder, cumin powder, oregano, cayenne and garlic and mix well.

2.   Add 1 to 1½ quarts cold fresh water just to cover the meat. Bring to a boil for one minute, then turn down the heat and simmer for 1½ hours.

3.   Add 1 to 2 teaspoons salt (taste as you add—the chili will sweeten with the addition of the salt, but you do not want it "salty").

4.   Make a paste of ⅓ cup coarse cornmeal and ⅓ cup cold, fresh water and stir until it is smooth. Stir the corn meal paste into the chili gradually. Simmer another 45 minutes .

5.   Serve the condiments separately, and let each diner dress their own bowl.

Contributor: Amos Miller

Symon's Tailgate Chili

2 pounds ground chicken
Olive oil
Salt to taste
2 cup onion, small dice
3 cloves garlic, minced
2 Serrano chiles, sliced into thin rings
1 Tablespoon smoked paprika
2 Tablespoons chili powder
2 Tablespoons coriander, toasted and ground
1 Tablespoon cumin, toasted and ground
1 teaspoon cayenne
1 bottle (12-ounce) beer (IPA if possible)
1 can (14½-ounce) petite diced tomatoes
1 can (15-ounce) cannellini beans, drained and rinsed
1 can (15-ounce) red kidney beans, drained and rinsed
2 Tablespoons brown sugar
2 teaspoon cocoa powder
2 cup plus 2 Tablespoons water
2 Tablespoons corn starch
7 ounce Greek yogurt
½ cup cilantro leaves, chopped
Chipotle hot sauce to taste

1. Heat a large Dutch oven over medium high heat and add 3 tablespoons of the olive oil. When the oil is hot, add the ground chicken with a large pinch of salt and brown on all sides, breaking up the meat into smaller pieces as it cooks. Remove with a slotted spoon to a plate and set aside.
2. Drain the fat from the pot, then place back over the heat and add 2 tablespoons of olive oil. Reduce the heat to medium, and add the onion, garlic, and Serrano with a small pinch of salt. Let the vegetables sweat for a few minutes, then add all of your spices. Toast them for about 30 seconds, being careful not to burn them.
3. Next add the bottle of beer, making sure to scrape the bottom of the pot well. Add the meat back in along with the tomatoes and both beans.
4. Stir in the brown sugar, cocoa powder and 2 cups of water, and reduce the heat to low. Season with some more salt and hot sauce to taste, and simmer stirring occasionally for 2 hours.
5. In the meantime, make the garnish by mixing together the yogurt and cilantro with a pinch of salt. Refrigerate until ready to use.
6. After 2 hours, if the chili looks a little loose, thicken it by mixing together the cornstarch and 2 tablespoons of water, then stirring it in when the chili is at a gentle boil.
7. To serve, ladle some of the chili into bowls, garnishing with a big dollop of the yogurt. Serves 8.

Contributor: Michael Symon

Slow Cooker Turkey Chili

1 Tablespoon vegetable oil
1 yellow onion, chopped
1 red bell pepper, chopped
2 pound ground turkey
3 garlic cloves, chopped
¼ cup tomato paste
2 cans (14½ ounces each) fire roasted tomatoes
1 can (15-ounce) black beans, drained and rinsed
1 can (15-ounce) kidney beans, drained and rinsed
1 cup frozen corn kernels
1½ cups chicken broth
2 teaspoons chili powder
1 teaspoon ground cumin
1 teaspoon dried oregano
½ teaspoon salt
½ teaspoon ground black pepper
Shredded pepper jack cheese, optional garnish
Diced avocado, optional garnish

1.   Heat the oil in a large skillet over medium-high heat. Add the onion and bell pepper and cook until tender, 8-10 minutes. Add the turkey and cook until no longer pink, 6-8 minutes. Add the garlic and tomato paste and cook 2 minutes.
2.   Transfer the turkey mixture to a slow cooker. Stir in tomatoes (with their juices), black and kidney beans, frozen corn kernels, chicken broth, chili powder, ground cumin, dried oregano, salt and black pepper. Cover and cook on high for 4 hours or low for 6 hours. Reduce heat to warm and serve out of the slow cooker.
3.   Garnish with cheese, avocado, and corn chips, if you like. Recipe makes 6 - 8 servings.

Contributors: Lauren Miyashiro; Kellie Kelle

California Gold Rush Chili

1 Tablespoon vegetable oil
3 pounds beef, cut into ¼ inch cubes
1½ cups white onion, finely minced
8 garlic cloves, finely minced
¾ teaspoon garlic powder
2 cans (15½-ounce each) chicken broth, fat removed
4 ounces tomato sauce
3 Tablespoons ground cumin
10½ Tablespoons mild chili powder
4½ Tablespoons medium chile powder
1 Tablespoon hot chile powder
2 teaspoons salt
½ teaspoon meat tenderizer
½ teaspoon light brown sugar
1 teaspoon hot sauce

1. In a large pot simmer onion and minced garlic in 2 cups of chicken broth for 10 minutes. Add tomato sauce and all dry spices, except the tenderizer and sugar. Mix well.
2. Brown the meat in vegetable oil using a separate pan and drain well. Sprinkle meat with tenderizer.
3. Add meat to the onion/spice mixture. Add remaining broth and simmer for 2½ hours.
4. Mix in brown sugar and your favorite hot sauce just before serving. Cool at room temperature, then top with cheese.
5. Put in an airtight container then freeze for about 2 months.

Contributor: Anonymous

Down Home Texas Ranch Chili

2 lbs ground beef
1½ cup water
2 teaspoons natural hickory smoke
1¾ cup diced white onions (set ¼ cup aside)
1½ cup chopped bell peppers
2 Tablespoons chipotle base
3 cups diced tomatoes in juice
¼ cup tomato paste
¼ cup bacon crumbles
2 teaspoons beef base
3 Tablespoons chili powder
1 teaspoon cumin
2 Tablespoons sugar
1 teaspoon cinnamon
2 cups kidney beans
1 cup black beans
1 cup shredded cheddar cheese

1.   In a large pot over medium-high heat, brown the ground beef, about 5-7 minutes, and drain excess liquid.

2.   Add all ingredients except the beans, ¼ cup diced white onion, and cheddar cheese to the browned beef, cover, and simmer for 30-40 minutes.

3.   Add beans and remaining ¼ cup diced white onions to chili and simmer for an additional 20 minutes.

Contributor: Anonymous

Mole Style Chili with Black Beans and Andouille

1 Tablespoon olive oil
1 large yellow onion, finely chopped
2 andouille sausages, about 6 oz. total, finely diced
3 zucchini, cut into ½-inch pieces
1 teaspoon ground cumin
1 teaspoon ancho chili powder
Coarse kosher salt and freshly ground pepper, to taste
2 cans (14½-ounces each) diced tomatoes with juices
2 Tablespoons minced canned chipotle chilies in adobo sauce
1 Tablespoon adobo sauce (from the canned chilies)
1 ounces unsweetened chocolate, finely chopped
1 teaspoons dried oregano
2 cans (15-ounces each) black beans, drained and rinsed

1.　A large, heavy pot over medium heat, warm the olive oil. Add the onion and sauté until it begins to soften, about 5 minutes. Add the sausages and cook until browned, about 5 minutes. Add the zucchini, cumin and chili powder. Season with salt and pepper and stir for 1 minute to toast the spices. Add the tomatoes with their juices, the chipotle chilies, adobo sauce, chocolate and oregano. Bring the chili to a boil, reduce the heat to medium-low and simmer for 10 minutes to blend the flavors.

2.　Add the black beans and simmer until the zucchini is tender and the flavors have blended, thinning the chili with water if it is too thick, about 10 minutes more.

3.　Taste and adjust the seasonings with salt and pepper. Spoon the chili into warmed bowls and serve immediately. Serves 4 to 6.

QUICK TIPS

Chipotle and ancho chili powder offer great flavor to recipes; keep them on hand for spicing quick-cooking recipes with little effort. Chipotle chilies in adobo sauce are available in cans in the Latin section of most markets. For a meatless version, omit the sausage. This chili improves overnight, so make it a day ahead, or look forward to the leftovers.

Adapted from Williams-Sonoma Weeknight Fresh & Fast, by Kristine Kidd

Greg's Groovin' Chili

2 Tablespoons vegetable oil
2 large onions, finely chopped
2 medium green peppers, finely chopped
3 stalks celery, finely chopped
8 pounds ground beef
1 can (6-ounces) tomato paste
2 cans (14½-ounces each) stewed tomatoes
2 cans (8-ounces each) cans tomato sauce
1 can (7-ounces) chile salsa
3 garlic cloves, finely chopped
4 Tablespoons chili powder
1 medium jalapeño chili, seeded and chopped
Oregano to taste
Freshly milled black pepper

1. Heat a heavy stew pot or large Dutch oven over medium-high heat. Swirl in enough oil to cover bottom of pot. Sauté onions, green peppers and celery just to soften, about 10 - 12 minutes. Add meat and cook 10 min or until brown, stirring all the while. Stir in all other ingredients.
2. Turn heat to low or medium-low, just to allow ingredients to simmer. Cook for 2½ hours, stirring frequently. Serves 14.

Contributor: Greg S. Marner

Devil's Dream Chili

1 Tablespoon oregano
2 teaspoons paprika
11 Tablespoons Gebhardt's chili powder
4 Tablespoons cumin
4 Tablespoons instant beef bouillon
3 bottles dark Ale
2 pounds pork steak, cubed
2 pounds chuck roast, cubed
6 pounds ground chuck
4 large onions, chopped
10 cloves garlic, minced
1 Tablespoon dried red pepper
¼ cup jalapeños, sliced
2 teaspoon coriander
1 Tablespoon Tabasco sauce
2 teaspoon Louisiana Red Hot Sauce
1 cup tomato sauce
1 Tablespoon corn starch

1. Using a heavy-bottomed pot or large Dutch oven, put in paprika, oregano, chili powder, beef bouillon, beer, and 2 cups water. Let simmer.

2. Working in bathes, brown meat In a large skillet with olive oil. Using slotted spoon, transfer each browned batch of meat to the Dutch oven. Never crowd the pan with meat. Too much liquid will be released and you will steam, not brown, the meat.

3. When meat is done, remove a little of the drippings, and sauté onion, garlic, and jalapeños. When onion is translucent and soft, transfer to Dutch oven. Stir in dried red pepper, sugar, coriander, Tabasco, red hot sauce, and tomato sauce. Bring to a boil and when boiling, immediately turn heat down so mixture simmers. Cook covered for one hour.

4. Dissolve corn starch in ¼ cup tepid water and add to chili, stirring well to blend .Continue to simmer for an additional 30 minutes.

Contributor: Susie Mann

Trantula Jack's Famous Chili

3 pounds cubed beef
2 medium sweet onions, finely chopped
3 large cloves garlic, finely minced
2 cans (10-ounce each) chicken broth
1 can (12-ounce) tomato sauce
1 can (12-ounce) diced tomatoes
1 can (14½-ounce) red kidney beans (optional)
7 Tablespoons chili powder
2 Tablespoons ground cumin
¼ teaspoon Tabasco sauce

1.   Sauté beef in skillet. Put beef into your favorite chili pot and simmer with onions, garlic, and broth for one and a half hours. Keep your hands off and leave the lid on!
2.   Add the tomato sauce, diced tomatoes, kidney beans if you're using them, the chili powder and the ground cumin. Stir.
3.   Add the Tabasco sauce and simmer for another 15 minutes. Add salt to taste.
4.   Serve with an ice-cold beer. This will serve 6-8 hungry folks.

Contributor: Jack Thompson

Uncle Clyde's Squirrel Chili

3 Tablespoons cooking oil
2 onions, chopped
3 pounds squirrel meat, coarsely ground
2 Tablespoons Worcestershire sauce
3 garlic cloves, minced
4 Tablespoons red chile, hot, ground OR
     4 Tablespoons red chile, mild, ground
2 teaspoons cumin
1 teaspoon oregano, dried, preferably Mexican
2 teaspoons salt
16 ounces kidney beans, soaked, rinsed and cooked
15 ounces chili sauce

1.   Heat oil in a Dutch oven or heavy 5-quart saucepan over medium heat.
2.   Stir in onions and cook until translucent. Add meat. Break up any lumps with a fork and cook, stirring occasionally, until meat is evenly browned.
3.   Add Worcestershire sauce and garlic and cook for 3 minutes. Stir in ground chile, cumin, oregano, and salt and cook, uncovered, for 5 minutes. Add beans and chili sauce and simmer, uncovered, for 1 hour.
4.   Taste and adjust seasonings. Serves: 10 to 12.

Contributor: Junior Trimmer

Mole Pablano Chili

3 large dried Pasilla chiles
1 dried California or Ancho chile
1 to 2 Tablespoons chipotle chiles in adobo
½ cup raisins or dried cherries
2½ cups dark beer or beef broth (or combination)
3 pounds organic beef brisket, cut into 1-inch cubes
    (or boneless pork picnic shoulder roast)
3 to 4 Tablespoons olive oil
1 teaspoon kosher salt
4 large Spanish onions, sliced
10 large cloves of garlic, minced
½ teaspoon ground cinnamon
2 Tablespoons chile powder
1 Tablespoons ground cumin
1½ teaspoons dried thyme
1 Tablespoon dried Mexican oregano
2 ounces organic unsweetened chocolate, like
    Dagoba
1 cup crushed tomatoes
2 or 3 cans (15-ounce each) black or pinto beans

GARNISHES

Sour cream or crema fresca (similar to mild sour
    cream)
Chopped fresh cilantro and scallion tossed together
Shredded jack or cheddar cheese
Crispy tortilla strips

1. Place Pasilla and California chiles in a microwave-safe bowl, cover with cold water, and cook on high for 2 minutes. Remove bowl from the microwave and set aside to soak for 20 minutes. When the chiles are soft, remove and discard the stem and seeds. Place chiles in a food processor or blender with ¼ cup of the soaking liquid, the raisins and ¼ cup of beer. Purée to a smooth consistency.

2. Season the cubed beef well with salt and black pepper. In a large, heavy bottomed sauté pan, over medium heat, warm 1 tablespoon of the oil. Add the beef and sauté until browned, about 15 minutes.

3. Heat 2 tablespoons of oil in a large Dutch oven over medium heat, add the onion and garlic. Season with salt and pepper and sauté for 10 minutes or until the onions are soft and tender.

4. Add all of the dried spices and sauté until fragrant, about 3 minutes. Add the chile purée, reduce the heat and simmer for 5 minutes stirring frequently so it does not scorch. Add a little beer if necessary. It will become a thick, aromatic paste. Add the chocolate and stir until melted.

5. Add the beef into the Dutch oven and stir well to coat, along with the remainder of the beer or broth and tomatoes; season to taste with salt and black pepper. Cover and simmer for 3 to 4 hours over low heat until the meat is tender. If the chili becomes dry, add more beer or water .

6. Add the drained beans. Taste for seasoning, adding more chipotle chile as desired. Simmer until the beans are heated through and the chili is the desired thickness, 30 to 45 minutes.

7. Serve with all of the fun toppings right away, or chill to reheat in a day or two. Serves 8.

Adapted from A Conscious Feast by Nicole Aloni

Vegetarian Chili

2 medium zucchini, chopped
1 medium onion, chopped
1 cup chopped green pepper
1 cup chopped sweet red pepper
3 cloves garlic, minced
3 Tablespoons olive oil
2 cans(28-ounce each) Italian stewed tomatoes, cut up
1 can (15-ounce) tomato sauce
1 can (15-ounce) pinto beans, drained
1 can (15-ounce) black beans, drained
1 jalapeño pepper, seeded and chopped
¼ cup fresh cilantro, minced
¼ cup fresh parsley, minced
3 Tablespoons chili powder
1 Tablespoon sugar
1 teaspoon salt
1 teaspoon cumin

1.   In a large pot, sauté zucchini, onion, peppers and garlic in oil until tender.
2.   Stir in all remaining ingredients.
3.   Bring to a boil.
4.   Reduce heat, cover and simmer for 30 minutes, stirring occasionally.

Contributor: MizzNezz

South of the Border Chili

4 large Idaho® potatoes
1 Tablespoon vegetable oil
12 ounces ground turkey
1 medium onion, diced
1 red or green bell pepper, diced
1 garlic clove, minced
1 Tablespoon chili powder
1 can (15-ounce) red kidney beans, rinsed and
    drained
1 can (14½-ounce) stewed tomatoes
½ teaspoon salt
2 Tablespoons grated low-fat cheddar cheese,
    optional
2 Tablespoons low-fat sour cream, optional

1.   Preheat the oven to 400°F. Wash the potatoes, pierce the skin a couple of times to help it release steam while baking. Place the potatoes directly on the middle rack, bake for approximately one hour or until internal temperature is 210°F.

2.   In large nonstick skillet, over medium-high heat, heat oil. Add ground turkey; cook, stirring to break up large pieces until lightly browned, about 5 minutes. With slotted spoon, remove turkey from skillet, set aside.

3.   To skillet, add onion, bell pepper and garlic, cook until vegetables are tender-crisp, about 4 to 5 minutes. Add chili powder; cook, stirring, 1 more minute.

4.   Stir in kidney beans, stewed tomatoes, ¼ cup water and salt. Bring to a boil and add the turkey, then reduce heat; simmer until thickened, about 10 to 12 minutes.

5.   Halve potatoes lengthwise, cutting almost to base of the potato. Mash slightly with fork, leaving in skins. Spoon chili mixture over each potato, dividing evenly. Top with cheddar cheese and sour cream.

Recipe by Idaho Potato® Recipes

San Antonio Chili Queens Chili

2 pounds beef shoulder, cut into ½-inch cubes
1 pound pork shoulder, cut into ½-inch cubes
¼ cup suet
¼ cup pork fat
3 medium-sized onions, chopped
6 garlic cloves, minced
1 quart water
4 ancho chiles
1 serrano chile
6 dried red chiles
1 Tablespoon comino seeds, freshly ground
2 Tablespoons Mexican oregano
Salt to taste

1.   Place lightly floured beef and pork cubes in with suet and pork fat in heavy chili pot and cook quickly, stirring often.

2.   Add onions and garlic and cook until they are tender and limp. Add water to mixture and simmer slowly while preparing chiles. Remove stems and seeds from chiles and chop very finely. Grind chiles in molcajete and add oregano with salt to mixture.

3.   Simmer another 2 hours. Remove suet casing and skim off some fat. Never cook frijoles with chiles and meat. Serve as separate dish.

Contributor: Institute of Texas Cultures - A Chili Queen Recipe

SOB Veggie Chili

¼ cup olive oil, divided
2½ cups diced yellow onions
1 poblano pepper, stemmed, seeded, and chopped
¾ cup diced red bell pepper
½ cup diced yellow bell pepper
1 large or 2 small jalapeño peppers, seeded and
 minced
2 Tablespoons minced cilantro stems
1 Tablespoon minced garlic
2 Tablespoons chili powder
1 Tablespoon Emeril's Southwest Essence
1 teaspoon ground cumin
½ teaspoon crumbled Mexican oregano
2 teaspoons salt, divided
2 cans diced tomatoes, with juices
6 cups Emeril's All Natural Organic Vegetable Stock
 or other low-sodium vegetable or chicken
 stock
2 cups cooked kidney beans, drained
4 cups diced (½-inch) zucchini
4 cups diced (½-inch) yellow squash
1 Tablespoon masa harina or yellow cornmeal
2 Tablespoons freshly chopped cilantro leaves
Sour cream, for serving
Grated sharp cheddar cheese, for serving
Chopped green onions, for serving
Fried tortilla chips or strips, for serving

1. Preheat the oven to the broil setting.
2. In a large Dutch oven over medium-high heat, add 2 tablespoons of the olive oil and Sauté the onion, poblano, red and yellow bell peppers until soft and lightly caramelized, about 6 minutes. Add the jalapeño, cilantro stems, garlic, chili powder, Southwest Essence, cumin, oregano, and 1½ teaspoons of the salt and cook, stirring, until fragrant, about 2 minutes. Add the tomatoes and vegetable stock, bring to a boil, reduce heat to a simmer and cook for 10 minutes. Add the beans and continue to cook at a simmer until the flavors come together, 30 to 40 minutes longer.
3. While the chili is simmering, toss the zucchini with 1 tablespoon from the remaining oil and ¼ teaspoon of the remaining salt and place on a large baking sheet. Broil until caramelized around the edges, 5 to 7 minutes. Remove from the oven and repeat with the yellow squash, remaining tablespoon of oil and remaining ½ teaspoon of salt. Set the zucchini and squash aside to cool while the chili is simmering.
4. Once the chili has simmered for about 40 minutes, add the zucchini, yellow squash, masa harina, and chopped cilantro and cook for 10 minutes longer. Taste and adjust seasoning, if necessary.
5. Serve the chili hot, with bowls of the sour cream, cheddar, green onions and crispy tortilla chips or strips for guests to garnish their bowls, as desired. Recipe makes about 2½ quarts.

Recipe courtesy of Emeril Lagasse

CHEF'S NOTE:
This chili is best made a day in advance.

EMERI

Hell House Chili

4 pounds ground beef
3 large onions , finely chopped
½ cup green pepper, finely chopped
5 garlic cloves—pressed
2 pounds crushed plum tomatoes
1 pound medium tomatoes, diced
3 cans red kidney beans with liquid
3 Tablespoons brown sugar
2 Tablespoons white sugar
8 Tablespoons chili powder
4 teaspoons cayenne pepper
1 teaspoon salt
3 Tablespoons bacon fat
1 bottle dark ale
2 Tablespoons garlic powder
6 ounces tomato paste

1.   In a large skillet, working in batches, brown meat, removing with a slotted spoon and putting in large heavy-bottomed pan or Dutch oven as you work. Drain off some fat and brown onions, green pepper, and garlic until onions soften, about 10 to 12 minutes. Add to Dutch oven with meat.

2.   Add remaining ingredients except tomato paste. Bring to a boil and when boiling, immediately lower heat to a strong simmer, and cook for one hour, covered. Stir and taste every now and then. After 30 minutes, add half the tomato paste. Cook for fifteen minutes, then check for thickness and flavor. If too liquidy or if you want a stronger tomato flavor, you can add the remaining paste with just enough water to thin, if it makes the chili is too thick.

3.   Serve with shredded cheddar cheese, Tabasco sauce, diced onions, hot chili oil, red pepper flakes.

Tolbert's Original Chili Parlor Chili

3 pounds lean beef
⅛ pound rendered beef kidney suet (if you want to go for it)
1 teaspoon ground oregano
1 teaspoon ground cumin
1 teaspoon salt
1 teaspoon cayenne pepper
1 Tabasco hot sauce
3 Tablespoons chile powder (optional)
4 hot chile peppers
At least two chopped cloves of garlic
2 teaspoons masa harina (or cornmeal, or flour)

1. Sear beef in a large soup pot or cast-iron Dutch oven. You may need a little oil to prevent the meat from sticking. When the meat is all gray, add suet and chile peppers and about two inches of liquid (you can use water, I use beer). Simmer for 30 minutes.
2. Add spices and garlic, bring just to boil; lower heat and simmer for 45 minutes. (NOTE: Add more liquid only to keep the mix from burning.)
3. Skim off as much grease as you can, and add masa harina. Simmer for another 30 minutes. Taste and adjust spices if necessary.
4. This is a spicy chili, so leave out some of the spicy stuff in the beginning if you have a tender tongue. At this point, I refrigerate the chili overnight which allows the chili to mellow and you can skim off all the grease.

Contributor: Frank Tolbert

Mexican Chicken Chili

1 Tablespoon olive oil
1 white onion finely chopped
1 can (15½-ounce) navy beans, drained and rinsed
1 can (15½-ounce) black beans, drained and rinsed
1 can (15½-ounce) northern beans, drained and
    rinsed
1 can (15½-ounce) whole kernel corn, drained
1 can (8-ounce) tomato sauce
2 cans (14½-ounce each) diced tomatoes with green
    chiles, undrained
1 packet (1¼-ounce) taco seasoning
3 skinless boneless chicken breasts cooked and
    shredded; or, 1 whole rotisserie chicken,
    shredded (about 4½ cups total)

1. Heat 1 tablespoon olive oil in a large pot over medium heat. Add 1 finely chopped white onion to the pot and sauté for about 5 minutes, until the onions soften and become translucent.
2. Stir in 1 (1¼-ounce) packet of taco seasoning.
3. Add half of a 15½-ounce can of navy beans, half a 15½-ounce can of black beans, and one whole 15½-ounce can of northern beans to a blender and puree.
4. Stir pureed beans to the pot.
5. Add an 8-ounce can of tomato sauce, two 14½-ounce cans of diced tomatoes with green chiles, and a 15½-ounce can of drained whole kernel corn to the pot.
6. Add about 4½ cups of shredded chicken to the pot. You can use leftover chicken such as rotisserie chicken or the meat of 3 cooked chicken breasts.
7. Mix in the remaining half can of navy beans and half can of black beans, then stir to combine.
8. Let your white bean chicken chili simmer over medium heat until fully heated through, about 15 to 20 minutes. Add juice of 1 lime and season with salt and pepper to taste.
9. Top with tortilla strips, shredded cheese, and sour cream to serve.
10. Corn tortilla strips OR corn chips, shredded cheddar cheese, sour cream.

NOTES

If you find the chili is not thick enough to your liking, take about a cup of liquid from the chili. Mix it with 1 to 2 Tablespoons of a thickening agent such as flour, corn masa flour, or cornstarch. Add the mixture back to the chili and slowly mix it in to thicken the chili.

Contributor: Isabel Laessig

Darkness Falls Chili

2 Tablespoons vegetable oil
1 large onion, chopped
6 cloves garlic, finely chopped
2 pounds ground beef
1 can (4-ounce) diced green chilies
1 can (4-ounce) jalapeño peppers
1 can (12-ounce) diced tomatoes
1 can (6-ounce) tomato paste
6 Tablespoons chili powder (or more if you like to
    breathe fire)
1½ Tablespoons ground cumin
2 Tablespoons apple cider vinegar
2 Tablespoons brown sugar
1 pound pinto beans, cooked and drained
Salt & freshly milled pepper to taste

1.   Sauté onion in vegetable oil in heavy-bottomed pot or Dutch oven. When onions are translucent, add garlic. Stir for 30 seconds then add ground beef, green chilies, jalapeños, tomatoes, tomato paste, chili powder, cumin, vinegar, brown sugar, oil and drained beans.

Fred's Mexican Fantasy Chili

1 pound of ground beef
1 diced green bell pepper
1 diced red bell pepper
1 diced white onion
1 cup diced tomatoes
1 cup pinto beans (optional)
2 Tablespoons cumin
1 Tablespoon garlic powder
2 ounces of chili powder
2 diced seedless jalapeño peppers
¼ cup of beer (optional)
1 cup of water
Salt and pepper to taste

1.   Sauté in a skillet with Crisco or olive oil the onions, red and green peppers and jalapeños for approximately 10 minutes.
2.   In a stock pot, brown your meat. When meat is cooked through, add onion mixture, diced tomatoes, water, beer, cumin, chili powder, garlic, salt and pepper. Bring mixture to a boil. Allow to simmer for about 30 minutes, stirring occasionally. Recipe makes 4 to 6 servings.

Contributor: Fred Garcia

Joe Cooper's Chili

3 pounds lean beef
¼ cup olive oil
1 quart water
2 bay leaves
8 dry chile pods or 6 Tablespoons chili powder
3 teaspoons salt
10 cloves finely chopped garlic
1 teaspoon cumin powder
1 teaspoon oregano or marjoram
1 teaspoon red pepper
½ teaspoon black pepper
1 Tablespoon sugar
3 Tablespoons paprika
3 Tablespoons flour or 6 Tablespoons cornmeal

1.   When olive oil is hot, in 6-quart pot, add meat and sear over high heat; stir constantly until gray—not brown. It then will have the consistency of whole-grain hominy.

2.   Add 1 quart water and cook (covered) at bubbling simmer 1½ to 2 hours. Then add all ingredients, except flour and cornmeal. Cook another 30 minutes at same bubbling simmer, but no longer, as further cooking will damage some of the spice flavors.

3.   Now add thickening* (either the flour or cornmeal), previously mixed in 3 tablespoons cold water. Cook 5 minutes to determine if more water is necessary (likely) for your desired consistency. Stir to prevent sticking after thickening is added.

NOTES

*Some prefer all flour, others all cornmeal, and still others use cracker meal—about as good, and more convenient. Suit your own taste.

Original West Texas Chili

3 pounds ground or cubed chuck
¼ cup oil
1 quart water
1 teaspoon salt or to taste
10 cloves garlic, minced
3 ounces chile powder
1 teaspoon ground cumin
1 teaspoon oregano leaves
1 teaspoon cayenne pepper—more or less
½ teaspoon black pepper
1 Tablespoon sugar
3 Tablespoons paprika
3 Tablespoons flour
6 Tablespoons masa (fine ground corn meal)

1.   In a large skillet, sauté meat in oil until browned. Add water and simmer 1½ to 2 hours.
2.   In a small bowl, mix salt, garlic, chili powder, cumin, oregano leaves, cayenne pepper, black pepper, sugar, and paprika.
3.   Add to skillet. Simmer 30 minutes. Cooking longer will cause spices to lose flavor.
4.   In a small bowl mix flour and masa. Wisk flour-masa mixture into chili, stirring constantly to prevent sticking.
5.   Bring mixture back to simmer until thickened. Remove from heat. Serve over beans, rice, hot dogs, enchiladas, burritos, or eat plain.
6.   Cheese (cheddar, longhorn, queso blanco, etc.) goes well on top. Recipe serves 6.

Slow Cooker Cactus Chili

2 pounds ground beef
1 large onion, chopped
2 cans (28-ounce each) diced tomatoes
2 cans (15¼-ounce each) black beans, drained
2 cans (15¼-ounce each) yellow corn, drained
1 jar (30-ounce) diced nopales (cactus)
1 can (8-ounce) tomato paste
3 Tablespoons chili powder
2 Tablespoons white sugar
1 chipotle pepper, chopped
2 teaspoons garlic powder
1 teaspoon ground cumin
1 teaspoon salt
1 teaspoon ground black pepper

1.   Combine ground beef and onion in a large skillet over medium heat; cook and stir until beef is browned, about 5 minutes.
2.   Transfer beef and onion to a slow cooker. Stir in diced tomatoes, black beans, corn, nopales, tomato paste, chili powder, sugar, chipotle pepper, garlic powder, cumin, salt, and pepper.
3.   Cook on low until flavors combine, about 4 hours.

Contributor: Denice D.

New Mexico Green Chile Chicken Stew

3 chicken breasts, cubed
1 Tablespoon olive oil
1 medium onion, chopped
4 medium potatoes, chopped
3 cans (14½-ounce each) chicken broth
12 large Hatch green chile peppers, diced
2 large zucchini, sliced
2 carrots, cut into pieces
1 teaspoon salt
1 teaspoon garlic salt
1 can (15¼-ounce) can whole kernel corn, drained
*   (optional)*

1.   Heat the oil in a large, heavy saucepan over medium heat. Cook and stir the chicken until browned, about 3 minutes.

2.   Add potatoes and onion; cook and stir until browned, 3 to 5 minutes more. Add broth, green chiles, zucchini, carrots, salt, and garlic salt.

3.   Bring to a boil; reduce heat and simmer until vegetables are tender, about 1 hour. Add corn and simmer until heated through, 10 to 15 minutes more.

Contributor: Ingrid

New Mexico Chili Verde

2 pounds pork butt, trimmed and cut into 1½-inch
    cubes
2 Tablespoons vegetable oil
2 cup onion, finely chopped
2 minced garlic cloves
1-2 jalapeños, seeded and diced
6 cups chicken broth
6 ounces beer (optional)
½ teaspoon oregano
1 teaspoon salt
1 teaspoon pepper
3 bay leaves
2 teaspoon cumin
1 can (10-ounce) diced tomatoes
3 large potatoes, diced
2 Tablespoons butter
2 Tablespoons masa (corn flour)

1.   To prepare the Hatch chiles, broil them in the oven, turning often to evenly darken skin, while making sure they don't burn.

2.   Remove from oven and cover with a dish cloth for 10 minutes to steam off the skins.

3.   While the chiles are resting, prepare the meat, sprinkle with salt and pepper and brown with onions and garlic in oil in a large pot for 5 minutes.

4.   Add jalapeños, broth, half a can of beer, and spices, bring to a simmer.

5.   Let simmer for 1 hour.

6.   Peel skin from chiles, chop and add to the pot (including the seeds).

7.   Continue to simmer for 30 minutes then add the tomatoes and potatoes (add a cup of hot water or broth if needed).

8.   Simmer until potatoes are done.

9.   Melt butter in a small skillet and add masa, cook for 2 minutes stirring constantly—add to the pot to thicken.

Submitted by Catalina Crawler

Our Last Word On Chili

Tips and Basic Methods for Making Chili

When it comes to chili, every cook has their own bag of tricks for making a brew so special that family and friends just can't seem to get enough. One so special that it may even become all the rage at that next chili cookoff. We hope the following pages will provide some basic information that proves helpful in making both newbies and the more experienced chili-heads even better at their craft.

TOOLS AND EQUIPMENT

Smallwares - While it may seem elementary, two of the most important tools for any cook is a good, sharp chef's knife for trimming and cubing the meat and chopping vegetables, and a sturdy cutting board on which to do that chopping. You'll also need a smaller kitchen knife for working with the chiles. Okay, so that's three things.

To complete your inventory of smallwares you'll need an array of bowls, both large and small, a couple of long-handle kitchen spoons for stirring and mixing, as well as a couple of ladles for skimming and serving.

Cooking Vessel - For cooking your chili, you'll need a large, heavy-bottomed pot. While some cooks use a traditional cast-iron pot, we recommend a 5½- or 6-quart enameled cast-iron Dutch Oven (lid not necessary), since plain cast-iron may react badly to acidic ingredients such as tomatoes. A heavy stainless steel or aluminum stockpot can work as well, so long as you're careful not to let the bottom of your chili burn.

Although certainly not traditional, those cooks whose schedule prevents them from being in the kitchen during long simmering times may want to utilize a slow cooker for cooking their chili. There are several excellent models on the market for under a hundred dollars. You'll find at least two recipes in this cookbook designed for slow cookers.

Blenders and Grinders - When it comes to making chili, nothing beats roasting and grinding your own chilies and herbs. To do this, you're going to need a blender and spice or coffee grinder to do the job. These grinders can cost anywhere from under twenty-five dollars to more than four hundred dollars. Just remember, more expensive does not necessarily equate to better.

For those cooks who are traditionalists, the mortar and pestle (or molcajete) and a little "elbow grease" will accomplish the same results, some say even better. A good selection of either is available for under a hundred dollars.

WHAT'S IN THE LARDER

Chilies - As you should already know, peppers are the backbone of any chili, as they add both flavor and heat to your brew. Our Guide to Chilies at the beginning of this book will provide all the information needed to select the right fresh or dried chiles for your project.

Onions - Generally speaking, white onions are the go-to onion for preparing chili, though a sweet yellow onion variety like Walla-Walla, Vidalia, or Texas Sweet is also nice. Substituting onion powder for the real thing is not recommended, as it will not provide the depth of flavor chili needs.

Garlic - Fresh, peeled-to-order garlic is the best way to go when it comes to making chili. Pre-peeled (if available) would be our second choice, while jarred whole, sliced, or minced in water or oil is a definite "no-no." If fresh is not available, a good quality granulated or powdered garlic can be used, although the flavor of your chili will definitely suffer.

Oil - It's important that you select a neutral oil such as peanut oil, canola oil, corn oil, avocado oil, or just plain vegetable oil for making your chili. Stronger flavored oils such as olive oil (especially extra virgin), coconut oil, and sesame oil will alter your chili's taste, and are therefore not recommended.

Cumin - An essential spice for any Tex-Mex and Mexican dish, cumin imparts a warm, earthy aroma, and a subtle citrusy flavor to your chili. For the maximum impact it's best to toast cumin seed and grind them in your spice mill. If using a pre-ground variety, check the "Use By" date to ensure it's as fresh as possible. Ground spices, if kept in a tightly sealed container in a dark cool place, have a usable shelf-life of two to three years.

Chili Powder - The best way to take your chili to the top is to make your own chili powder, as explained in our Chili Guide at the beginning of this cookbook. Commercial chili powders usually contain and array of other spices and salt. If a recipe calls for chili powder and you don't want to make your own, we encourage you to read the label to ensure you're getting pure, unadulterated Chile powder.

Other Ingredients - Additional spices you should keep on hand include dried basil Leaves, Mexican oregano, paprika, coriander, bay leaves, thyme leaves, and cinnamon. Fresh parsley and cilantro are also must.

Your pantry should be well-stocked with a variety of beans, both dried and canned (although chili purest consider beans heresy). Also, diced and whole canned tomatoes (forgo crushed as you can easily crush your own), tomato sauce, and tomato paste.

Keeping your pantry, spice rack, and fridge stocked with these ingredients will help ensure not having to make a supermarket run every time you're overcome with the urge to make your favorite pot of chili.

BEEF, PORK, POULTRY, OR . . .

The two most important ingredients needed in making chili are the chilies and the protein you select. Most people, at the mere mention of chili, think of a peppery, tomatoey beef concoction. And while beef is unequivocally the most popular protein in the chili world, it is by no means the only workable choice. Let's examine a few.

Beef - A recent Loupe survey indicated that two-thirds (66.8%) of Americans prefer beef chili over those made with other proteins. In fact, four of the top four chili styles are made with beef.

When choosing beef (about ¼ to ⅓ a pound per serving), look for cuts with an 80/20 lean to fat ratio, such as short ribs, chuck roast, or brisket. After all, fat is favor. You'll also want to consider texture. Do you want your beef in chunks, chopped, coarsely, or finely ground.

Poultry - For a lighter chili with fewer calories, think about substituting ground turkey or chicken for beef. You can still utilize many of the same ingredients as in beef chili.

Or make a "white chili" by using diced chicken or turkey breast, forgoing the tomato, and using a white bean such as Great Northern or cannellini. Either way, your chili will contain less than half the calories of beef chili.

You'll find several versions of turkey or chicken chili recipes within the pages of this cookbook.

Vegetarian - Depending on which survey you prefer to look at, there are between four and ten percent of Americans that identify as vegetarian. And since many vegetarian chili recipes are heavy on beans, they're loaded with fiber and protein. Did you know that ½ cup of beans has as much protein as one ounce of meat? It's true.

Pork - Just about any recipe for beef chili can be made with pork. While most pork chili recipes call for pork shoulder, you can make it less fatty by using cuts like pork loin or pork tenderloin. You can also use it coarsely ground or cubed, allowing ¼ to ⅓ of a pound for each serving. Either cut or style of pork you choose will pair well with fresh chiles and makes a wonderfully delicious brew.

The next time you're searching for a different chili, give the New Mexico Chile Verde recipe found in the recipe section. You'll be glad you did.

Game and Other Meats - Whether farm-raised or the kill of a hunt, the meat from practically every mammal or edible foul—venison, elk, bison, goose, duck, lamb or goat—can be used to make a fantastic chili. Just be aware that some of these meats are very lean, making it necessary to add some bacon or other fat to prevent them from drying out. Don't be afraid to experiment.

Regardless of which meat you choose, it's important that you brown it on all sides to give your chili a deeper, richer, more flavorful foundation. After browning your meat, remove and cover it to rest and stay warm. Then add your spices to "bloom" while the onions soften. This will awaken their essential oils, thus bringing out their full flavor. Deglaze your pot or Dutch Oven with beer, stock, or water before returning the meat and adding the other ingredients.

Good chili has to cook low and slow in order for the flavors to meld. This is accomplished by letting it simmer uncovered for one or two hours over medium low heat, stirring occasionally to prevent the bottom from burning. Covering your chili pot causes condensation which will drip into your chili that can dilute the flavors you've spent all day creating. Just add a little more liquid if your chili starts getting too thick. On the other hand, thin chili can be thickened by adding a small amount of slurry made from masa harina corn flour and water.

Chili Sides and Toppings - Chili is always better when accompanied by a nice selection of sides and toppings.

For serving, chopped cilantro, shredded cheddar and/or jack cheeses, sour cream, sliced green onions, sliced radish, pickled jalapeños, and lime or lemon wedges are a must.

For sides we recommend tortilla chips, crackers, and one or two different kind of cornbread. You may even consider a jicama coleslaw or roasted corn and black bean salad.

Remember there's no such thing as a bad chili. So don't be afraid to experiment and by all means have fun. Our hope is that you find the information and recipes within these pages helpful as you venture into the world of chili.

Made in the USA
Coppell, TX
01 April 2025

47744085R00040